THE THREE
— of —
CHRIST

TREVOR DENNIS

First published in Great Britain in 1999

Society for Promoting Christian Knowledge
36 Causton Street
London SW1P 4ST

Reprinted once
Reissued 2009

British Library Cataloguing-in-Publication Data
A catalogue record for this book is available
from the British Library

ISBN 978–0–281–06119–8

1 3 5 7 9 10 8 6 4 2

Typeset by Pioneer Associates, Perthshire
Printed in the UK by CPI Bookmarque, Croydon, CR0 4TD

Produced on paper from sustainable forests

THE THREE FACES
— of —
CHRIST

The Three Faces of Christ was originally published in 1999 as Trevor Dennis's third collection of stories and poetic reflections on biblical passages. It was preceded by *Speaking of God* (SPCK, 1992) and *Imagining God* (SPCK, 1997). Since then SPCK has published two further collections, *Keeping God Company* (2002) and *God Treads Softly Here* (2004). Trevor Dennis started preaching through storytelling in the 1970s, when he was a school chaplain, but most of his published pieces, including those contained in this book, were designed primarily for adults. For nearly twelve years he taught Old Testament Studies at Salisbury and Wells Theological College, and SPCK has published four books of his that explore Old Testament narratives. In 1994 he joined the staff of Chester Cathedral, where he is Vice Dean. He has continued to write on the Bible, producing a children's Bible, *The Book of Books*, for Lion/Hudson in 2003, and *The Christmas Stories* in 2007, followed by *The Easter Stories* in 2008 (both for SPCK). He is married to Caroline, and they have four children and two grandsons.

CONTENTS

INTRODUCTION

Let us dare to speak of God, needing to pluck up our courage, not because we are afraid, but because we know our words will quickly fail, and can at best but touch the hem of God's mystery; and because in speaking of things so close to our heart and soul, we will give ourselves away.

Let us dare to speak not of God's high majesty and power, for such speech is altogether too predictable and we are up to our necks in it already. Too easily it makes God remote and ourselves afraid. Let us speak instead of matters more often kept secret, I mean God's smallness, his vulnerability and pain; God's shyness, his playfulness and laughter, and the comfort she draws from our love. (Let us not always refer to God as 'he' and 'him'. Let God sometimes be 'she' and 'her', for then we might lose our fear and the deference that keep her at arm's length and learn more quickly to enjoy her company.)

Let us speak of God in Christ, God small enough at first to lie in our arms, God a dead weight, so it seems, as we lower him down from a cross. Let us go first to Bethlehem, to catch again the child in ourselves and the everlasting child in God. Then let us take the short road to the darkness of Golgotha, to enter God's loneliness, and to discover not only the workings of his salvation, but how we might still soothe his face. And after that let us be drawn gladly to resurrection, and back to the Garden of Eden. The story of our expulsion from Eden has left us with an eternal longing to return. Well, let us go there, and see what mysteries await us!

And so, beyond the sound of God's pain, let us hear God's feet dancing and the music of her saxophone, and, in a side street in the heavenly city, let us find her up to her elbows in flour, ready nonetheless to embrace us. That divine embrace will be the making of us.

THE THREE FACES OF CHRIST

Blessed art thou,
O Christmas Christ,
that thy cradle was so low
that shepherds,
poorest and simplest of earthly folk,
could yet kneel beside it,
and look level-eyed into the face of God.   (Anon)

> J. Morley, ed. (1992), *Bread of Tomorrow: Praying
> with the World's Poor*, SPCK, Christian Aid

What you must first understand about the face
   of Jesus
is that it is so small.
He has no hair yet.
His milk teeth are not yet showing beneath his
   gums.
His lungs are well developed,
as Mary and Joseph and the animals have already
   discovered.
But he has no language beyond his crying.
He, the Word of God,
cannot say 'Mamma'.
He, the Son of God,
cannot call him 'Abba',

let alone argue with rabbis and priests in the
    Temple
the finer things of heaven.
He is the Love of God,
and yet he cannot smile
(though sometimes, when he gets the wind,
his face crumples up as though he can).
His eyes cannot focus,

and yet, and yet,
if you kneel beside his manger
(you will be far too high above him if you stand),
if you kneel so that your face is close to his,
then you will find yourself
looking level-eyed into the face of God.

*   *   *

A second feature of his face to have imprinted
    on your soul,
the laughter lines that play about his eyes.
Some keep their Christ pickled in piety,
or paint him stern as a schoolmaster,
in Dickens,
on a bad day,
unbending, uncompromising, unforgiving,
Why then is he such good company?
Why does he tell such stories?
Why does he teach the lame

not just to walk but dance the tango?
Why does he turn water into wine,
and speak of living life to the full?
Why does he bend so low,
this 'unbending' man,
that he can wash disciples' feet?
Why will he always compromise,
if that means touching someone in their need?
Why is forgiveness his Alpha and Omega,
his beginning (his middle) and his end?
Why does he fill his own tomb with such
    merriment
that we can only call it 'resurrection'?
See, his whole face dances with the laughter
    lines of God!

*   *   *

The third marking of his face you cannot miss.
I mean the pain,
the bewilderment,
the sorrow,
the sheer anguish of it.
Such is the expression we have left him with,
now we have strung him up on that heavy
    cross beam
he has lugged along these narrow streets to
    Golgotha.
He will die with it.

His hair is hidden behind black thorns.
His teeth are gone,
knocked out in the beating the soldiers have
    given him.
His lungs rasp for breath and soon will lose
    the fight.
We have robbed him of his language, too,
left him just a few last words
with which to hurl his loneliness at heaven.
He cannot smile,
for we have wiped all smiling off his face.
His eyes can hardly see for pain,

and yet, and yet,
if you stand yourself beneath his cross
(oh, do not kneel, or bend your head, but raise
    your eyes and see!),
if you stand on very tip-toe,
then you will find,
to your great sorrow,
but his small comfort,
that you can reach
to soothe the very face of God.

2   THE SHEPHERD'S TALE

There were shepherds living in the fields, keeping watch over their flock.   (Luke 2.8)

We see your coaches driving down from Jerusalem to Jericho, stopping off for souvenirs at the 'Inn of the Good Samaritan'. You take the old road, then stop to clamber up to the cross on the ridge overlooking the Wadi Qilt, with its view of the hills of the desert and the Monastery of St George, of Jericho one way and Jerusalem and those wretched settlements the other. We come to sell you trinkets, or we let you sit in one of our black tents for a few shekels, while your guide tells you about our way of life. You smile at us and in ten minutes, with your guide's help, try to understand us. Outside you listen to us piping our sheep and goats down to the water in the bottom of the wadi, and get quite carried away, or you laugh behind your coach windows at the television aerials standing by our tents. But you don't really take much notice of us. For you think we are not sophisticated like you. We live on or beyond the edge of civilization, you suppose, because you equate civilization with your own lifestyle and think Wise Men come from the West. Nomadic people have always been in receipt of others' contempt, ever since those others decided to settle down and build walls and call the land their own. We have always seen things differently, and not played your games. You have never trusted us.

But I will tell you the truth. We live closer to the earth than you do, and that means closer to heaven, also. We know every line of the earth's face, and every star by name. Our ancient stories say we have been here since light first came upon the earth. So it was hardly surprising that we recognized again the light of Creation when it shone that night over Bethlehem. It was the light of the First Day, when God said, 'Let there be light!' It was the light of Eden and the Burning Bush, the same light as shone later on a mountain of Transfiguration and on the morning of Resurrection. We knew the angels' song, too. We had heard it at the world's beginning, when the morning stars sang together, and all the angels shouted for joy. We well remembered that ancient joy of heaven, and so naturally we went to Bethlehem to join in the party.

Do not despise us. We have been here a long time, and have seen and heard what you all long for. Listen to the earth! Look for the light of creation! Keep your ears open for the joy of heaven! Bethlehem, small and unremarkable, caught between the desert and grand Jerusalem, did not come as a surprise to us, nor that simple crowded home, nor the young couple and the child, new born in the hay, wrapped in its warmth against the winter cold. None of that surprised us. For we have been here a long time, and have always kept close to the earth, and known the rhythms of heaven.

Yet you may find it all strange, too simple, too tucked away out of sight, too smelly, and far too ordinary.

It was not too ordinary for us, thank God!

THE ANGEL'S TALE

Jacob had a dream. See, a stairway stood upon the earth! The head of it touched the heavens, and see, messengers of God going up and down upon it!
(Genesis 28.12)

Suddenly there was with the angel a multitude of the heavenly host, praising God and saying, 'Glory to God in the highest heaven, and on earth peace among those whom he favours!' (Luke 2.13–14)

I saw you when you were first made. I saw your very making. I watched as God took the clay in his bare hands to form a man. I watched again as he took that man's side and built it into a woman. I saw the delight in his eye. I saw the intimacy with which you were made, and knew it was the intimacy for which he created you. I recognized that intimacy, for I had enjoyed it myself since before creation. I thought you would always possess it. But you slipped out of God's hands, lost yourselves, and lost him also. You forgot his touch, the play of his breath on your face, the beat of his heart against yours. You took to imagining he was trapped in heaven, above the solid barrier of the firmament, while your feet were set too firmly on the earth. God in heaven and you on earth, and never the twain shall meet. That is what you believed.

9

So one day we set up a stairway reaching from earth right up to heaven. Jacob saw it at Beth-El. Its stairs were not empty. It was full of us angels, ascending and descending upon it. Heaven was speaking to earth, for we were God's messengers, and carried in our bulging pockets his secrets and his love letters addressed to you. More than that. God came down that stairway himself. Jacob that night found him standing beside him. Jacob that night heard him say he would never leave him.

Jacob heard and saw the truth. The stairway between earth and heaven remained, and still it stands. Still we go up and down it, about the same business. Still the door of heaven stands open. And still God comes down it himself and stands beside you. Still he reminds you of the ancient intimacy of Eden. Still he promises never to leave you. And his generosity is just the same. Remember, Jacob was up to his neck in deceit and cruelty when God met him at Beth-El. He had nothing but the hatred of his wronged brother behind him, and ahead a long journey to an uncertain conclusion. He was not good enough to meet God. We never are. But God came to him nevertheless. It is his way. We never deserve his coming.

Yet you forgot that stairway. It opened heaven wide and brought God down to earth, but your eyes were not open, as Jacob's were. You fell back into the old ways of imagining a great gulf fixed between you and God. You made life very lonely for yourselves, and for

God also, for your company means so much to him.

Then came Bethlehem, and the cry of a new born child in the quietness of the night, and that carnival in heaven. The mayhem was our doing. All heaven was let loose! The world had not seen such a thing since it was made! The morning stars remembered the song they had sung then, and declared ours even finer. Quite a compliment!

And no-one saw, no-one heard, except a few bedouin keeping it in turns to watch their sheep and goats. All heaven let loose, and hardly anyone noticed! It was and is passing strange.

THE WISE MAN'S TALE

After Jesus was born in Bethlehem of Judea, wise men from the East came to Jerusalem. (Matthew 2.1)

We were used to the delights of high table, the Georgian silver, the attentive waiters, the feasts to mark special occasions, the wines, each carefully chosen by the Steward to suit its particular course, the decanters of port and madeira, the Latin graces, the portraits against the oak panelling, the intricacies of the beamed roof, the brilliant conversation, and the talk over coffee in the Senior Combination Room afterwards.

Such a scene was duplicated many times over in the various colleges of the university. It was a golden age. Yet even in such a place, at such a time, we were famous, for each of us was a Nobel prize winner twice over. And three of us in one college! Not that we saw as much of each other as you might imagine, for each of us was in demand throughout the world. We lived half our lives in aeroplanes, in hotels, in other people's universities, in conferences and large, packed halls with people hanging on our every word. Our books were discussed not just in learned journals, but on television shows. Most of our invitations we had to refuse. Each of us in his or her way was teaching the world to see itself differently, so we were told. Together, people said, our visions spelled an intellectual revolution of the significance of the Renaissance or the Enlightenment. Absurd talk, but not unpleasant!

Why, then, did we slip away together one day, leaving behind our high table and our books and word processors, and go to Bethlehem? I cannot tell you, except that our life-long search for truth compelled us. To be precise, it drove us to Jerusalem, to the Hebrew University on Mount Scopus. There, we somehow imagined we would reach our destination. They listened to us, then told us we had not yet arrived, though we did not have far to go. They were very helpful, though for some reason they would not accompany us on the final stage of our journey.

The next day we walked the few miles to Bethlehem. They put us on the right road. I do not know why we walked. We could have taken a taxi, of course, but that did not seem appropriate. At the road-block near the edge of the town the soldiers regarded us with obvious suspicion. 'We're not used to pilgrims on foot,' they said. They body-searched us, questioned us for half an hour, then let us through. It was the first time we realized we were on a pilgrimage. We did not seem to share the piety of the pilgrims we had come across in Jerusalem. We had thought them too organized, too credulous, too caught up in all the razzmatazz. We had seen them trotting after their guides like children, going to one holy site after another, constantly supplied with holy thoughts and told to think them. We were surely after some larger truth than that.

And so we were. And we found it in Bethlehem. For there we met a child, a small child, very small, a baby, a few days old, and older than creation. There in Bethlehem we rediscovered the laughing child within ourselves, and, for the first time, against all our old, carefully nurtured expectations, found the child in God. We brought him our learning, our cleverness, our genius as it was called, and gave them to him as all we had to offer. He received them most graciously. He could see the gladness in our eyes, and wanted nothing more.

We met some local bedouin who had got there before us. As they embraced us, it seemed we had known them for a lifetime. They took us to their tents and gave us the most wonderful feast we had ever had. We sat outside beneath the bright stars, and kept long silence together. There was a bond between us which could never be broken, and a shared wisdom which could never be lost, for we had met Truth in its entirety and its eternal simplicity, and had been deep-warmed by the very Love of God.

THE SOLDIER'S TALE

Herod sent and killed all the children in and around
Bethlehem who were two years old or under.

(Matthew 2.16)

I won't keep you long. I've plenty I could tell you, but
I can't bear to think of the words for most of it.

We were only obeying orders. We were at the end
of a long chain of command. The wrong end.

Killing children is not all that peculiar. We weren't
the first, and weren't the last, either. Jericho, Auschwitz,
Cambodia, Bosnia, Rwanda, Darfur . . . Bethlehem. It's
all the same. Except that we were told to leave the
adults alone and any children over three. The other places
were worse than that, and the killers weren't so choosy.

Some of us got quietly drunk before we started.
The only way we could cope. We had orders only to
take the little ones, as I've said, though we had to give
some of the women a right beating to get their babies
from them and get them off our backs.

When we'd finished, they loaded us into trucks to
take us back to Jerusalem. I was dead lucky. They put
me in the last one, right at the back of the convoy.
Half way back I jumped out. The others didn't move
when I got out. 'Good luck,' the corporal said, and
gave me a bit of a shove, and that was that.

17

I knew the lie of the land. I had been brought up nearby, see. The desert was close. They'd never find me there, I thought. I knew some of the bedouin. They'd give me shelter and a change of clothes, and enough food and drink to get me to the border.

They did too. Then the rains came in buckets in the hills, and the wadis got full of water. When I climbed down into one, I'd strip off my clothes and wash myself all over. But I could never get myself clean. It felt as though the blood of those babies had soaked right through my skin, and I'd have it all dark and spoiled inside me till the day I died.

Still, after a bit I made it to Egypt. I tried to disappear, but the faces of those babies still followed me. In the end I couldn't take it any more, so I decided to go back and give myself up.

On the way I bumped into a young woman and her husband. They had a child with them. He was very small, still a baby really. I couldn't keep my eyes off him, though God knows I tried.

'Where are you from?' I asked.

'We had to escape from Bethlehem a while ago,' they said. 'There was a terrible massacre. All the children under three, killed. Can you imagine? We got out by the skin of our teeth. We're not going back. We're finished with Bethlehem. Going up north instead, to Nazareth.'

They saw me looking at the baby and noticed the look on my face. The mother hesitated. She suddenly realized I'd been a part of it. I'm sure she did. But then she said (you won't believe this), 'Do you want to hold him for a moment?' And before I could say anything, she put him in my arms.

So many of us deserted after the massacre, they've stopped looking for us. Least, that's what they say. I work in Ramallah now, an Arab place north of Jerusalem. There was trouble in the town the other day. I expect you read about it in the newspapers. Some things they didn't tell you, though. The soldiers were using high velocity bullets that explode inside you. See this scar? A doctor and I were bending over someone who'd been shot. He was bleeding heavily. We were right inside a room on the fifth floor of a block of flats. The soldiers must've been using telescopic sights, and they can't have missed our uniforms. We were wearing white coats, after all. But they shot at us all the same. One of their bullets hit the doctor smack in the head. I just got shrapnel in the back and in my shoulder. Another team went up for the man we'd been trying to help, and somehow they managed to get him out, and the doctor and me as well. The man's still alive. The doctor isn't, of course.

I will fight and work for justice until I die. That baby on the road from Egypt, and his mother, they showed me what I had to do. Showed me I was for-given, too. I could feel it strong, when she handed him to me and I held him in my arms. It was like holding the fire of God.

6   THE FEAR OF GOD

They went out to the Mount of Olives . . . and went to
a place called Gethsemane.   (Mark 14.26, 32)

Jerusalem had too much religion for its own good,
certainly at times of festival. Too many pretensions,
too much intolerance. Too many people believing
they were right, too many vested interests, too many
people clinging on to power, and a temple that was far
too grandiose.

Jerusalem was a desert town, on the very edge of
wilderness. Around the Sea of Galilee, and beside the
banks of the Jordan river to the north and south of it,
the countryside was lush. Reed beds and great marshes,
full of birds and their singing, flower meadows, antelope up in the hills, hyrax among the rocks, and black
and white kingfishers diving into the shallows around
the edges of the lake.

Jesus was on his own, up in the hills of the Golan,
with the lake shining silver over to the west. Behind
him on the high plateau antelope grazed among stately
white storks. The steep hillside where he was sitting
was clothed in its finest robes of spring flowers, wild
lupins, yellow scabious, tall acanthus, and mysterious,
exquisite arum lilies of a deep maroon velvet. Small

21

birds were everywhere, finches, buntings and warblers, while in the ravine to his right vultures and eagles slid past the nesting ledges on the easy grace of wide wings. He recognized all that beauty. He had seen it before in Eden.

'They are not afraid of us up here,' he said. He had come to converse with his God. 'They are not afraid. We do not pose any threat to these flowers and birds, nor to the animals or rocks of these ancient hills. We are at home here, God, my friend, and always welcome. It will not be so in Jerusalem at Passover. It will not be so in Jerusalem.'

Of course, Galilee was not all beauty. Jesus knew tenant farmers and their families hanging on by their fingertips, praying for their foreign landlords to leave them alone, but never having their prayers answered for very long. He knew other families which led an even more precarious existence, the men going down early to the market places hoping for work a day at a time, often returning empty-handed. He had met many bent double by debt, slavery, illness, or grief, others split by loneliness, or by unrequited longings for a child. And then there were his friends among the Pharisees, fighting for the very survival of their ancient Jewish faith against the paganism and disdain or hatred of the surrounding world.

How could he leave all this, all of them behind? He knew he would not return.

He could no longer see the lake. It had disappeared

behind a fall of rain. He got up, took in deep the scent
of the flowers, and started off for the track that would
take him back to his friends. No doubt he would get
soaked to the skin before he reached them.

*   *   *

It was true. They were not welcome in Jerusalem.

The air was brittle with fear, and the place swarming
with soldiers. The fanatics had brought their own
brand of violence as their contribution to the festival.
Fights had broken out, and five soldiers had got killed.
The Romans had decided they would have to teach
the Jews another lesson. Then there was the incident
in the Temple.

Two Pharisees came running to warn Jesus that the
Temple authorities and the Romans were planning to
make an example of him. They should get out quick,
go up and over the Mount of Olives, and into the
desert the other side. There were people there who
would look after them till the festival was over, and
things were back to normal. Then it would be safe for
them to make their way to Galilee again.

They hurried along some back streets. It was dark,
and they were not noticed as they went out through
the crowded gate in the city walls. They ran down into
the little valley of the Kidron, and began to climb the
Mount of Olives. They came to a garden called Gethsemane. The shadows were dark under the old olive
trees. His friends scattered and lay down, suddenly

exhausted, though they had not come far. Jesus himself stood looking across to the Temple gleaming in the moonlight the other side of the valley. It was so vast! Not so much a city with a temple, as a temple with a city attached.

'It is too grand for you, my friend,' he said quietly to his God. 'It is designed to put the fear of you in the hearts of the little people who come here, and it does its job too well. What is more, amidst all that grandeur, all the fine terraces and porticos and flights of steps, they have hidden you away in a cupboard. They have put you behind a curtain, and left you there to spend your time in the dark, on your own, with one visit a year from the High Priest. What madness is that! What madness to try and hide you away, when you ride on the wind that blows free across these hills, when you shine in the high stars, and rise each morning above these slopes and turn the stones to gold. How dare they say you give audience but once a year, and only to someone as high as a High Priest! They have made you a recluse and a snob. I will show them! I will take you, my friend, back into that city and we will turn it upside down, you and I, in our own inimitable way. We will bring you out of their hiding, and teach them that no-one need be afraid of you. We will remind them of the Garden of Eden, before the man and woman there grew so frightened. We will teach them that love casts out fear and sends it spinning over these desert hills and down into the depths of the Dead Sea where it belongs. They have no reason to be afraid. We will teach them that, you and I.

'See, they are coming to meet us. So grown up with their swords and their clubs. Such determination in their stride. Such bravado. Yet they seem like small children, lost and bewildered, missing their mother.

'What will they do to us, do you think? What will they do this time? They threw us out of Eden long ago. Now they have come looking for us, with torches and swords and spears and clubs! Madness, all madness!'

He turned and went about among the trees shaking his friends awake. 'We are not going into the desert, after all,' he told them. 'I cannot turn my back on all this fear and hopelessness. They are coming to fetch us. We will go to meet them. As we always have.'

THE FRIENDS OF GOD

While Pilate was sitting on the judgement seat, his wife sent word to him, 'Have nothing to do with that innocent man, for today I have suffered a great deal because of a dream about him.'   (Matthew 27.19)

Moses soothed the face of the Lord his God.
(Exodus 32.11 – a literal translation of the Hebrew of the opening words of the verse)

'Take off your tunic.'

Her slave woman looked at her with horror.

'Take off your tunic,' she repeated. 'If I go through the streets in all this finery, I'll be spotted at once. I need to be inconspicuous. Take it off, woman. I'll need your cloak, too.'

'But what shall I wear?'

'Just take it off. You can think of that later.'

Still with the horror on her face, Rachel did as she was told. Claudia slipped out of her own tunic, and put on Rachel's. She went to go out of the room. She turned at the door. 'Wear my tunic, if you like, and go and have some fun with the other slaves.' Rachel stood there unable to move.

Claudia wrapped the cloak about her head and went out into the courtyard.

27

She had told Pilate the man was innocent. Her sleep had been disturbed all night by fearful dreams about him. 'The man's a troublemaker,' had been her husband's reply. 'He's a Jew, isn't he? And even if he is innocent, just listen to the crowd outside! They're baying like hounds! I have to satisfy their blood lust or we'll have serious trouble.'

'So you are just going to throw him to them, so they can tear him to pieces?' she had replied.

'Of course not. They're not allowed to execute him. We'll have to do their dirty work for them, as usual.' He had gone across to the window. 'He's a threat to the state, and that's all there is to it.'

'And all there is to *him*?'

'Yes.'

'But the man's *innocent*! Do you want an innocent man's blood on your hands?'

'I'm up to my knees in innocent men's blood already! How do you think I survive in this God-forsaken place! How do you imagine I keep the peace? Anyway,' he had added, 'I have washed my hands of this particular man's blood. I did it in front of the crowd. Declared my innocence before them all. Went down rather well, I thought. Now get out woman, and leave me in peace.'

Thus their conversation had ended. Soon after that she had heard the distant sounds of the beating the soldiers had given him. She had thought they were going to knock the life right out of him. But they

were masters of their trade, and knew when to stop.
She had heard their mockery, also, and known the
truth of it. At no point, however, had she caught sight
of the man. She had to see him before he died, this
strange man of her terrible dreams.

That was why she was now dressed in the tunic and
rough cloak of one of her slaves, following the crowd
to the quarry outside the walls where they were going
to crucify him.

She was not used to being on her own in a crowd
and felt very lonely. The streets were narrow. She was
pushed and shoved, and when a man coming out of a
doorway bumped into her, she tripped and fell. People
started walking over her as if she was part of the pave-
ment. For a dreadful moment she thought she might
be trampled to death, when two women knelt down
and quickly lifted her up onto her feet. They held her
by the arms, and the three of them were swept on
together, slowing as they got near the gate through the
walls. There the crush nearly took Claudia's breath away.
Her legs and back burned where they had been
stepped on. Eventually they were through, and soon
they found themselves on the edge of the quarry where
the uprights of three crosses were already in place.

The two women were still beside her. They watched
as the soldiers on crucifixion duty went about their
business. A larger number of soldiers stood facing
them and the other bystanders. The soldiers by the
crosses were experienced men. They had done it

before many times and prided themselves on their skill. They soon had them up. They picked up their tools and tackle, and marched off. The crowd pushed forward. The soldiers let a few people go up to the other two crosses, but they maintained a tight cordon round the one in the middle. One of the women who had helped Claudia approached the centurion in charge. Claudia could just hear her talking to him in a thick northern accent that marked her as a Galilean. It was clear the officer was refusing her request. The woman persisted. The officer shouted at her, and still she stood her ground. She said something to him Claudia did not catch, and one of the soldiers struck her hard across the face and knocked her to the ground. She lay there for a moment, and then began to struggle to her feet.

Claudia strode forward to the centurion. 'Do you know who I am, young man? I will report you to my husband Pilate. I will see to it that you are on the next boat from Caesarea. You will be sent to Britain I shouldn't wonder.' Mary of Magdala looked at her wide eyed. The centurion ran his eyes down her slave's cloak and tunic. 'Pilate's wife are you, lady? Pleased to meet you. And I'm the bloody Emperor!' He laughed and the soldiers with him. Their merriment mixed with the more usual sounds of crucifixion.

The two women turned away.

'I knew you weren't a slave,' Mary said. 'But are you really Pilate's wife?'

'Yes. Claudia.'

'And you come *here*?'

'Yes.'

Mary gazed at her, and shook her head. 'I am Mary, from Magdala, and this is Salome. We are old friends of his. You are welcome here, sister. As much as anyone is welcome in this place.'

Those were the last words they said to one another for several hours. The soldiers forced them to keep their distance. They could do nothing but watch. They wanted to wipe the blood from his brow, but they could not. They wanted to offer him something to drink, but they were not allowed to. They wanted to weep, but somehow the tears would not come. They were powerless even to cry. And they were mute, also, quite unable to speak. There were no words for it in any case.

The soldiers shifted from one foot to the other. Those who had come to mock this fine 'King of the Jews' had tired of it and gone home. Dark clouds came from the west and hid the sun. An icy wind blew. The very ground shivered. Then it went darker still, as if behind the clouds the sun had turned to ashes. The women peered through the gloom.

All of a sudden they cried out. There was a man beside the cross! Not one of the soldiers. A stranger. He had a ladder with him! They saw him climb a few rungs and start to wipe Jesus' face with a cloth. He was speaking to him, very softly, but they could hear every word.

'I did this once before, my friend,' the stranger said. 'Do you remember? On Sinai, when you saw the calf they had made and heard them call it their "god"? Do you remember? I soothed your face then, and now I have returned to do it again. Another rejection, and an even crueller one, my old friend. Only I find no anger in your pain this time. Let me wipe your tears again, my friend, my dear friend, my dearest God.' With shaking voice he began to sing, 'Arise, my love, my fair one, and come away. For see, the winter is past, the rain is over and gone. Arise, my love, my fair one, and come away...'

The soldiers were still facing the women and saw and heard nothing.

'Moses!' Mary whispered. 'It's Moses. Dear God! Moses!'

Jesus took a gulp of air and split the clouds open with his last cry. Then his head fell forwards, and Moses bent to close his eyes. At that moment the centurion turned round and looked, and saw.

At long last the women were able to weep. Mary and Salome wept for the man who meant so much to them, and for the hopes and dreams which had surely died with him. Claudia wept for herself and for the years of emptiness; for her husband who had sent this man to his death; above all for the God she had at last encountered.

'We must begin all over again,' she said.

SALVATION

A meditation on Isaiah 35.1–4 and 8–10

If by chance
you wish to hear of salvation,
do not send for a preacher.
Find a poet.
Isaiah will do.

The wilderness and the dry land shall be glad,
the desert shall rejoice and blossom;
like the crocus it shall blossom abundantly,
and rejoice with joy and singing.
The glory of Lebanon shall be given to it,
the majesty of Carmel and Sharon.
They shall see the glory of the Lord,
the majesty of our God.

I have walked, too briefly,
in the dry Judean hills,
always in winter,
or too early in the spring,
too soon for the swathes of flowers
that turn the land to blue and yellow,
red and purple.

And yet the last time
we found the desert crocus of which Isaiah speaks,
and other flowers I could not name,
delicate, exquisite,
glances of divine beauty
in the crowd of stone and rock,
promise enough of things to come.
We caught the desert in her pregnancy,
near to full term,
near to birthing
of a most astonishing beauty.
We stood and could imagine.

A few days later
there was no need for imagining.
At Gamla, high in the Golan Hills,
we found a more dazzling profusion of flowers
than most of us had ever seen.
We were there at the right time, exactly.
We had stumbled upon Eden.

Flowers speak so quietly.
They do not cry or lift up their voice,
or make it heard in the street.
They do not bully or cajole,
or drown us out with noise.
Flowers make no noise at all,
and yet their speech compels us;
they tell so clearly that God has passed this way.

Poet Isaiah does not speak of Gamla,
but takes us with him in his mind's eye
to the lush, poppy-strewn slopes of the
    Carmel ridge,
and into the forests of Lebanon,
and the coastal plain of Sharon,
and in a few lines,
in so few words,
gives all their fine fertility to the desert,
and says to us,
'There is your salvation!'

You see?
You need a poet,
when it comes to talk of salvation!
And where will he take us next?
To Auschwitz.

Strengthen the weak hands,
and make firm the feeble knees.
Say to those who are of a fearful heart,
'Be strong, do not fear!
Here is your God.
He will come and save you.'

Hands hanging down,
feebly signalling despair;
knees stumbling, falling,
revealing brutality,

and evil beyond reckoning
pressing down upon the chest.
Waking after fitful sleep
the limit of ambition;
no way out,
except in the queues to the gas chambers,
except on the lip of the death pits,
except on the charged wires of the fence,
except in the noose, if they decide to make an
    example of you.

The poet we call Isaiah
lives there himself.
He knows the hopelessness,
the fear,
the futility,
the wasting away,
the gasping for death.
'Do not fear!' he cries.
Words designed for kings before battle
are whispered by this poet in the huts
in the shivering dark of the night,
in broad daylight, passed down the line at
    roll-call.
'Do not fear! Do not fear!'
Royal language for those treated like slugs
    beneath the jack-boot.
'Here is your God!
He *will* come.'

He, the poet,
can hear the thud of the guns,
the rumble of the tanks,
the marching of feet
coming for liberation.
He can see God at the gate of the camp,
with his helmet at an angle,
and pockets full of food and medicines.
You see?
You need a poet
if you wish to hear of salvation.
'Strengthen the weak hands,
make firm the feeble knees!'
Oh yes!
Hope where there was despair,
compassion where there was brutality,
holding the head high,
where before there was only stumbling to an
    untimely death.
There is salvation!
Nothing soft,
nothing namby-pamby,
no half measures,
no cheap grace,
no cloying piety.
Instead, a God walking through the gate
that has so long been shut.

And finally the going home.
No cattle trucks this time,
nor suffocating heat,
nor dying on one's feet.
A straight, smooth road!

A highway shall be there,
and it shall be called the Holy Way;
the unclean shall not travel on it,
but it shall be for God's people;
no traveller, not even fools, shall go astray.
No lion shall be there,
nor shall any ravenous beast come up on it;
they shall not be found there,
but the redeemed shall walk there.
And the ransomed of the Lord shall return,
and come to Zion with singing;
everlasting joy shall be upon their heads;
they shall obtain joy and gladness,
and sorrow and sighing shall flee away.

The stumbling, falling mass of the camp
has become a carnival procession!
No enemy planes to bomb them,
no snipers' guns,
no land mines,
but a straight, smooth road,
built for the purpose,
for carnival,

for singing,
for homecoming!

And where is God
in this fine procession?
Riding in his heavenly staff car?
That is not his way.
He has no car,
and would not use it if he did.
No, there he is!
in the middle of the cavalcade,
carrying that child on his shoulders,
bouncing her up and down,
Rachel,
who came so close to death back in the camp.
There he is!
his arm round the waist of old Aaron,
who lost a leg to gangrene,
practising with him
for the three-legged race
at the next Passover,
and going like the clappers!
There he is!
holding the hand of Rebekah,
who lost everyone behind the wire,
parents, husband, children.
There is salvation for you!

You see?
For talk of salvation
only a poet will do.

What this particular poet could not see,
was a God inside the camp,
with lice in his hair,
and sores on his legs,
and the food missing from his belly.
Nor could he dream
that one day we would call *that* salvation,
and would need one Friday evening
to lift God's body from a cross.

No poet can say everything.

EDEN

'Truly I tell you, today you will be with me in Paradise.'
(Luke 23.43)

They did not know that the Garden of Eden lay just outside their city walls. The garden only belonged to their storytelling. It had never been a place of pilgrimage. (Mythical creatures called cherubim armed with a sword as sharp as lightning had made sure it could not be that, for they had been posted by God himself to bar all entrance to it. Their story said so.) The Garden was of a time before time, when snakes could talk, when God walked upon the earth and his footsteps could be heard, and when immortality was still a possibility. It seemed but a dream. It was not plotted on any maps. It could never be fixed in any spot, so people could say, 'Here it is!' It was a place beyond all boundaries, a place, perhaps, deep within the soul, a source of longing and hope, a reminder of a long-lost intimacy with God, a garden of the noblest and purest desire, a garden where once God's laughter was heard and shared. But that was all.

They did not realize it was so very close. Admittedly, it was not recognizable as a garden any more. Long ago it had gone to rack and ruin. Yet it had never been built over. It had never been used for any purpose. No-one had ever lived there, nor even gone there. People did not know why. It was not cursed land, nor was it declared sacred. They did not recognize they were avoiding it. They simply found themselves going elsewhere, in other directions, without knowing why, or even realizing what they were doing. It was simply overlooked.

Till one evening, when a young man was taken down from a cross. As his friends carried his body to the tomb they could not see where they were going, for their eyes were full of tears. Behind their little procession came two more. Two thieves had been crucified with the young man and needed burial. The mother of the young man had observed that neither of them had anyone to mourn them. So she had wrapped them up in the ample shroud of her grief, and gathered enough of her son's friends to bear their bodies also.

The young man had died in the end not of pain, not of the suffocation of crucifixion, nor of exposure or humiliation, but of abandonment. God's desertion had killed him. God had been closer than breathing all his life, but at the moment when he needed her most, she had seemed to desert him. On the cross he had been unable to find her. He had called out to her, and had been met with silence. He had listened for her footsteps, but had heard nothing. He had not been able to feel her breath upon his cheeks, and the stench of death had left no room for her scent. He had felt utterly alone, entirely rejected. That had killed him.

So now they carried the burden of his loneliness to his resting-place, though whether there could ever be any rest for him after a death like that, they did not know. Behind him came the bodies of the two thieves. The young man had spoken to one of them before he died, and that man's corpse was curiously light to carry. He had died well. Hanging on a cross, naked, with his genitals at the eye level of those watching, racked with pain and fighting for every breath, he had died well and in peace. His face said so as he was carried to his tomb. The body of the other thief, how-ever, was still twisted by a terrible agony. *Rigor mortis* had set in with strange and devastating swiftness, and his corpse was so distorted it was very difficult to carry. But he too was worth much grief, and much care. The young man had taught his friends to give special heed to those whom others rejected and despised, and to bestow dignity wherever it was denied. And so they took his body also down from his black cross, wrapped it in a shroud, and joined it to their sad procession.

They did not see where they were going, nor quite what they were going to do when they got there. A tomb was ready for the young man. But where would they bury his two companions? They did not know. They would see to it when they got there.

But they missed their way. Stumbling blindly in their grief, they entered the ruins of Eden. They did not realize where they were. Their footsteps fell soft along lines of paths last trodden by God in a time before time. They passed no cherubim, no flaming, whirling sword. The story had been wrong. The entrance was not guarded. There was no gate, no barrier of any kind. It was as if the place had been waiting for people to walk into it. No-one had ever come, that was all.

They found no tomb prepared in the place, of course, since they had lost their way. It was getting dark. What could they do? They could only leave the bodies behind in their shrouds, resting on the ground. They found two trees in the middle of the place, and left them at their feet. As soon as the Sabbath was over, they would return and see to things properly.

So they went quietly away, leaning on one another, still blinded by tears or numb with shock, back to an empty world, still not knowing they had been in Eden, nor what they had done.

For they had performed a most remarkable deed. In losing their way they had brought God back to Eden! And there, through the darkness of the night he lay, not with the first man and the first woman of the ancient story, but with two slaves who had been caught stealing from their masters, and whose cruel deaths had been meant to serve as an example to others.

Thick cloud covered the whole of that night. The moon did not rise. No stars shone. The sun did not rise the next day either. There was no dawn at which the birds might sing. The world was empty.

Another night passed.

The young man's friends got up early, before the morning came, to return to where they had left the bodies. Was this the way they had gone? It did not seem so, yet Mary of Magdala's sense of direction could be relied upon. She was sure they were going the same way as before. What, then, was this most beautiful garden? Where in the name of heaven had it come from? Its air was full of the scent of flowers and bursting with the song of birds. The last time they had smelled or heard nothing, except for the smell of death and the sound of their own footsteps. Had their senses been so dulled with shock and grief? And why, why this joy welling up in their souls? Why suddenly did the world seem so fresh and full of hope? Why were they so overcome? Where had their grief gone? It was just as if they were back in Eden!

They reached the two trees in the middle of the garden. The bodies were not there! Of course not. How could death be found in such a place? In that garden there was only room for life. 'This *is* Eden!' they cried, and at that moment they heard through the birdsong the new laughter of God. They recog-nized it at once, for it was the same as the laughter they had known in Galilee, the laughter the young man's mother had first heard in Nazareth, and had always loved so much. It was unmistakable.

They heard the laughter of two others also, the merry laughter of two men who had been born to slavery and had lived with it all their life, but now were free.

Tears filled their eyes, but they were tears of joy, of joy, of joy. Beneath the trees they joined hands, picked up their heels and danced.

THE HARROWING OF HELL

He descended into hell.   (From the Apostles' Creed)

I reached the tomb as the sun rose above the horizon. The stone was rolled away to the right, and the rays of the dawn shone inside. Afraid, bewildered, I entered where we had laid him such a short time before.

He had been so heavy to bear. We had carried far more to that tomb than the weight of his thin body. All the world's grief, all its ancient sadness we had taken to put down in that small, dark space, and the world's stupidity, also, as well as its brutality and lust for power which had at last defeated him, or so we then supposed.

It was over.

Now I was there again, with a new day's sun painting the tomb's yellow walls. Yet, as I bent my head and stepped inside, I found a black darkness still present. For there was no end wall to this tomb! Where rough hewn rock should have been, there was nothing! Or rather, there were the beginnings of an abyss that might go on for ever. I could not see whether it did or not, but it seemed in my terror, as suddenly I tripped and fell, that I would never stop falling, and that the dark would go on and on, world without end.

As I fell, I cried out, and to my surprise and immense relief an answer came at once. Soft light flickered round me to break into the dark, and then (thank God!), there were arms beneath me, catching me, holding me, and hands putting me gently on the ground, setting me on my feet, and steadying me.

'Where am I? And who are you?' I asked.

'You are in hell,' the angel said.

'In hell? What do you mean? But it is so quiet here! As if it is empty.'

'That is because he is far ahead of us. Most of his work is already done.'

'He is here? Is he alive, then?'

'He is Life itself. Do you wish to follow him?'

'It is dark, and I do not know which way to go.'

'I will lead you. Hold on to me, for deep sorrow clings to this place still, though he has passed on before us.'

'But surely he belongs in heaven, not here.'

'That is why he is here. Come, my friend, you will be safe with me. We will follow after him.'

I had not got up that morning to be led by an angel down the passages of hell. But there was, of course, no turning back. We went on together. It was so very quiet! We made no noise as we passed, and I would have heard every moan, sigh, or cry of anguish, had there been any. But there was only silence, silence and the deep sadness of which the angel had warned me. She put her arm across my shoulder.

'Will his joy never take over here?' I cried.

'Never,' she said. 'It does not belong here. Once his work is done, this place will be no more. The tunnels will collapse, and all the pain they once knew. These vile cells and their terrible loneliness will disappear, and there will be none to rebuild them.'

To right and left a series of narrow cells were let into the walls of the passage. Each one was different from the next. Each had known its own unique kind of misery.

'Was great evil here?' I asked.

'No. Only its consequences.'

'No cell is opposite another, and the walls between them are so thick! They could have had no sight nor sound of one another. Their loneliness must have been complete. How very terrible this place is! Not at all what I had imagined. Far worse.'

I stopped and hid my face in my hands. The angel knelt to comfort me. After a while she said, 'We must find him soon, or I too will find this place past bearing. I do not know how he dared come here on his own.'

We went on, clinging now to one another. The doors of the cells were all open. Not a single one of them was occupied, not till we reached the end of the last tunnel. And there he was, inside the final cell! He looked very near exhaustion. He was not alone. There was a man in the cell, and a young child. Christ had the child tightly by the hand. They were standing

opposite the man. I recognized him at once. We all
know that face and its ridiculous small moustache.

'Her name is Leah,' Christ was saying to him. 'She
was only three, when you packed her off to die in one
of those camps, of which you were so proud. Her
parents died, also, because of you, as well as her grand-
parents and all her aunts and uncles and cousins. Only
her brother is left. Her name is Leah. You must let her
take you out of here. She knows the way. She is very
wise for her years. She will lead you, and when you
are out of this terrible dark, I will find you myself and
take you home. For the moment, goodbye, my friend.'

Christ bent down and kissed Leah. 'You are perform-
ing a deed of the greatest heroism, and of a generosity
straight from heaven,' he told her quietly. 'There will
be much joy there today.' He kissed her a second and
a third time, and let her go.

The child took the man's hand and led him out past
where we were standing. When they had gone, Christ
broke down and wept.

'But surely,' I whispered to the angel, 'Christ cannot
let him go! Not after all he has done! Not just like
that!'

'But it was not "just like that". Did you not see the
child?'

'Of course I saw her! It was appalling! Christ using
her like that for his own purposes! Had she not suffered enough?'

'Then what are Christ's purposes?'

'Letting people like him go scot-free, it seems!'

'And did you not see the child?'

'Of course, I've just told you.'

'I do not think you did.' The angel turned. 'I must go to him now.'

She went across to Christ and held him as he wept. Left on my own I was suddenly overcome with shame.

'I would rather you were overcome with love, but your shame can be a start,' Christ murmured, 'and your strong arm. Will you help me out of here? My work is done now, and my strength is almost gone. This place will soon collapse beneath the weight of its own grief. We all need the clear air of resurrection, where we can breathe and laugh again. There is no room for laughter here.'

And so it was, that with an angel supporting him on one side, and me on the other, Christ came out of hell into the light of resurrection. It was done. He had finished. Soft echoes of alleluias came to us on the breeze of heaven. Soon they would surround us and shake all creation.

THE WALK TO EMMAUS

And they heard the sound of the Lord God walking to and fro in the garden in the breeze of the day.
(Genesis 3.8)

The Lord appeared to Abraham by the oaks of Mamre.
(Genesis 18.1)

Now on that same day two of them were going to a village called Emmaus.
(Luke 24.13)

He began as a stranger,
one who happened to be going in the same
    direction,
a pilgrim, they presumed,
returning from Jerusalem,
from a Passover lost in grief and overtaken by
    death.
He began as one they thought must live in a
    world of his own,
cut off in empty loneliness,
or else plain stupid.
He became on the way their companion,
their teacher,
at home their guest,
their host

(for *he* took bread and blessed and broke it),
their priest
(for the meal was no ordinary lunch),
and finally,
with eyes opened,
their God.

Have you ever heard of such a thing?

Yes, once in Eden,
and again by the oaks of Mamre.

For once in Eden,
in the Garden he planted,
near the place where grew a tree weighed down
      with knowledge,
and another with enough life to overcome death,
at the centre of the Garden
God came walking,
and the hearts of the man and woman burned
      within them,
and they too came to know their foolishness.
Each of them had known God's intimacy at their
      creation,
God's hands upon them,
God's breath on their faces,
God's warm, passionate kiss of life.
Later, near the Tree of Knowledge,
near the neglected Tree of Life,

they knew his intimacy again,
as he came walking in the cool of the day,
with footsteps they could hear upon the Garden's
    gravel paths.
But that story ended differently,
not with recognition,
for they knew him already and were afraid,
not with him bending low
to come inside their tent, as at Mamre,
not with him sitting cross-legged beside their fire,
nor with the breaking of bread, as at Emmaus,
nor with blessing, nor the surprise of joy,
but with expulsion and estrangement.
We speak of a loss of innocence in Eden,
and so there was.
Yet there was a larger loss of intimacy,
the intimacy of those acts of creation,
the intimacy we were made for.

On the road to Emmaus,
in a small house,
in a room,
at a meal,
that ancient intimacy was found again.
 We call that rediscovery
'resurrection'.

Some of it was played out long before,
beneath the oaks of Mamre,

where Abraham sat,
and Sarah worked,
when God came out of the heat of the sun,
without announcement,
without ceremony (beyond the usual hospitalities),
and sat and ate roast beef and mounds of cakes.
It was a return to the old intimacy,
the intimacy for which we all were made.
It was a moving on, also,
to hope beyond imagining,
and grief was turned to joy.
For there was new birth,
a new life beyond all expectation
(for Isaac was born when Sarah was ninety years
    of age and Abraham one hundred,
or so the story goes –
stories of resurrection are like that.)
Yet there was no moment of recognition.
Even at the story's end Abraham did not know
    his guest's identity.
Though the stranger knew his wife's name,
without any telling,
promised a child,
without hesitation,
gave the date of birth,
heard Sarah's silent laugh,
Abraham never tumbled to him,
never said, 'My Lord and my God!',
never went running to his friends,

never spoke of resurrection.
Maybe Sarah realized,
but the oaks of Mamre do not tell us so.
Their story remains unfinished,
waiting an ending.

At Emmaus,
in a smoky room,
over a meal,
at the breaking of some bread,
at a moment of eternal simplicity,
when the guest became,
without any rudeness or presumption,
the host,
then it found, that ancient story,
a proper conclusion.
Emmaus was made into Eden,
the flaming sword blocking all entrance
revealed as a figment of our guilt and fear-filled
    imagination.
The old intimacy was recovered,
seen and felt for what it was,
and this time shared in resurrection.

What ending does our story come to now?
Might we feel God's hands upon us,
God's breath upon our faces,
God's kiss?
Might we find hope beyond all imagining,

and grief turned all to joy,
new birth,
new life beyond all expectation?
Might we tumble to it all,
and know that we have stumbled upon
    resurrection?

I cannot answer that.
But I can assure you
that God tried to teach Abraham and Sarah
to prepare for surprises.

BEING IN CHARGE

The Lord God planted a garden in Eden, Land of Pleasure, and God took the human beings he had made, the man and the woman, and set them in the garden, to work it and watch over it.   (Genesis 2.8, 15)

And the man said, 'This is a wonderful place! It's got every sort of tree you could imagine, and some you couldn't! Look at the swathes of flowers, meadows with more kinds than you could count, all buzzing with insects! The trees are hanging with sloths and koalas, there are badgers digging underneath the rhododendrons and foxes sliding through the undergrowth, and the elephants are having a whale of a time in the lake – as are the whales (funny having whales in a lake in the middle of a garden, but this is Eden, after all)! As for the birds, the sky is huge with their song! This is a marvellous place, and I can lie here all day under the trees, and watch all this luxuriance around me and generally luxuriate, and get a bit poetic when the mood takes me, and when I feel hungry, I can just stretch up and pick another mango, peel another banana, or take a nice juicy apple perhaps.'

'I thought God said something about work,' said the woman.

'You can do that,' said the man. 'I can be the one to make sure you do it properly. You do the work, and I'll do the watching over.'

'But that's not fair!' cried the woman.

'Perfectly fair,' replied the man. 'You do the work. I'll take the responsibility. What could be fairer than that?'

'A lot!' said the woman.

'In fact,' continued the man, ignoring her, 'in fact, my responsibilities will be so large, that you'll have the better part of the deal.'

At this point God intervened, and agreed with the woman.

'You keep out of it!' shouted the man, who was getting far too big for his boots.

*　　*　　*

So God did keep out of it, or rather was kept out of it, and life for the man and woman changed. The garden went to rack and ruin, and soon they found themselves in a different world altogether. Life became a struggle to survive, a round of continual toil, a not knowing where the next meal was coming from. Thorns and thistles grew thick in the fields, and the woman had children round her feet all day long, as well as their crying in the night. Both of them were worn out.

One evening she and her husband were sitting disconsolate on the veranda. The sun was setting, and the sky was an extraordinary mixture of reds and oranges, purples, greens, yellows, blues and greys, but they saw none of it.

'This is ridiculous,' she murmured.

'What is?' asked the man.

'All this wanting to be in charge, and keeping God out of things.'

'I don't want to be in charge.'

'Of course you do. Ever since that time in Eden, when you talked of me doing the work and you having the responsibility, you've wanted to be in charge. And you've wanted to keep God out of things, and you've succeeded. And look where it's got us! Do you remember what it was like, the garden God made for us? It was *wonderful*! Who knows what we might have done with it, us and God? Once you got so full of your responsibilities, you decided it was too small. But you didn't know how large it was, did you. There were whales in the lake, for God's sake! Do you know how much space whales need? Only you didn't think. You didn't think. Just went on your own merry little way, and to hell with the consequences! Well look at the consequences!'

She was angry now, and her anger gave her new energy. 'Come on!' she cried. 'We're taking the kids, and we're going back to the garden to talk to God!'

'What about?'

'You know what about. About including him in things, instead of keeping him out all the time. About cooperating with him for a change. He is the creator, after all! Well, we can be pretty creative, too, and if we add our creativity to his, goodness only knows what this world might become!'

'But can't I be in charge any more?'

'No. God doesn't play at that game, so you'd better give up trying yourself. He needs us, and we need him, and that's all there is to it. Come on!'

She picked up the baby, got the other children in order, and started off in the direction of Eden. She turned her head. 'You coming?' she called.

THE GARDEN REVISITED

'Arise, my love, my fair one, and come away. For now
the winter is past, the rain is over and gone.'

(Song of Songs 2.10–11)

'Can you hear anything?'

The air was perfectly still. Not a leaf, not a blade of
grass moved. A field away a cow snorted, and half a
mile beyond a fox barked twice. An owl had been
calling earlier, but now was gone.

'Listen!'

'What?'

'You can hear the stars!'

They fell silent and remained so for a long time.
They put their arms round each other for comfort
and for warmth, though the night was not cold.

They had decided to come back in the dark, for
safety's sake, just in case.

'Will it really be any safer at night?' he had asked.
'After all, the darkness is not dark to her, it's as bright
as day for her, just like light. I've heard that somewhere.'

'Psalm 139, verse 12.'

'But are you sure it will be safer?'

'Don't know,' she had replied, 'but the flaming
sword should show up for miles in the dark. That
should tell us something.'

'What bleedin' sword?'

'*Flaming, flaming*! Stone me, don't you remember? When we left, there were these mythical creatures, and a dirty great sword, all on fire and whirling about all over the place, put at the entrance, so we couldn't get back in.'

'Oh yes, I remember now. Why were the mythical creatures on fire?'

She had hit him. Not very hard.

'Doesn't sound very welcoming, does it,' he had said. 'Mythical creatures, and a flaming sword, and all that whirling about here there and everywhere. Should we really try to go back?'

But they had not been able to help it. There are some rare places, perhaps just one place, to which we feel we must return, and for them the Garden of Eden was such a place. So there they were, in the dark, with their arms tight round each other, listening to the stars, on the edge of Eden, wondering. They could see no Cherubim, no sword, no fire, not even a notice warning trespassers they would be prosecuted. There was no fence to nail it on, nor any gate.

'Do you think they got bored waiting, the Cherubim?' he whispered. 'Or perhaps their sword went out, and they've had to go and get it lit again. A bit like the Foolish Virgins and their oil.'

'Maybe we imagined them, because we were so frightened,' she said, 'and the sword, the fire, the danger, the whole lot. Maybe we've been able to go back all this time. Maybe there's been nothing to stop us, except our fear, and our guilt.'

'What do you mean?'

'I don't know. Not until we're inside. Come on.'

They remained a moment longer, and then a moment still. Two owls sang in duet in the far distance, and another cow shook its breath across the field behind them. Nothing else.

They entered the Garden.

At once it was familiar. It was the place where they belonged. They were made for each other and for that place. They knew it immediately. It was their home. Being outside it had always felt not right. They had pretended to one another and to themselves that that was not the case. They had bought a nice three-piece suite, and curtains to match, and made the place where they lived their own. But that was precisely the trouble. They had been on their own. They had missed her company. That is why they had come back. To find the Gardener. To see if there was any chance of . . . To find the Gardener. That would be enough.

At once it was both familiar and wonderfully strange, for this time it was safe. They had left it before in fear. They had come back in some fear, also, but all fear was gone as soon as they dared set foot inside. They found the canoe where they had left it, those many years before. They pushed it out from the bank of the river, and paddled their way slowly towards the centre of the Garden. The rings left in the water shone gold. One, two . . . one two. The paddles swung in easy, gentle rhythm. The river curved away to the left, and they bumped the canoe gently into the bank and climbed out. Ahead were the two trees, the Tree of Life and the Tree of Knowledge. They put their arms round each other, suddenly unsure what to do. The trees held so many memories for them.

'What's that?' she said. The two trees grew beside one another, and some of their great branches intertwined. Where they did so, there was a curious dark shape.

'It's a tree house!' he answered. 'A tree house! Well I never did!'

'No,' she replied. 'But *she* did!'

'Who?'

'The Gardener, of course.'

'Do you think . . . ?'

'Let's see.'

They went forward and stood beneath the trees.

'What shall we say? "Anyone at home?" sounds silly.'

'Yes.' She paused. 'Kiss me.'

'What?'

'You heard me, silly. Kiss me.'

'Yes, but . . .'

'No buts. Kiss me. Oh well, if you won't, I will!' She took him in her arms.

A rope ladder snaked its way down from the tree house, and a merry laugh broke above their heads. A familiar voice rang out. 'Are you any good at climbing?'

'You bet we are!'

'Good! Welcome home, my friends! I've been on my own for quite long enough.'

THE FOOTSTEPS OF GOD

They heard the sound of the Lord God walking to and fro in the garden in the breeze of the day.

(Genesis 3.8)

Once upon a time, in a garden, in Eden, in a story about growing up, at the time when we had just begun and were first learning what it meant to be human, a man and a woman, only just emerged from boy and girl, heard the footsteps of God. Some people do not notice that little detail in the story. Others do, but fail to be astonished. Some, however, full of amazement, wonder what the sound can possibly have been like. They keep their ears open, waiting to hear it again.

The man lying on his own in the double bed is listening for it in the small hours of the night. He lost his wife last year, but he has still not been able to part with the bed they shared for so long. He hears the slow, mournful whine of the lorry coming to sweep the gutters of the road, and then, later, the clatter of the bottles on the milk float, and the soft clunk of the pint on his doorstep. Otherwise, all is quiet. The sound he longs for does not come. He supposes God's footsteps would sound much as his wife's used to, but he is beginning to forget what those were like. Soon it will be time to get up and feed the cat.

The priest raises the body and blood of Christ above the fair linen cloth on the altar. There is a rare moment of silence in the church. The stillness wraps her round, and she holds the disk of bread above the chalice longer than usual. She waits and listens, and thinks she hears something, only it is very faint. Then someone coughs, and she sees everyone is looking at her. Her face turns pink, and she begins the Lord's Prayer. The moment has passed.

The young man puts down his pint and leans on the table. His mates are laughing about something, but he is not concentrating any more. He was the life and soul a moment ago. It is the same every day after work. Down to the pub and a pint or two before catching the train home. Nothing heavy, nothing serious, nothing too revealing. Hide behind the jokes and the glasses of beer. Give nothing, or very little, away. This particular evening, he is suddenly caught with loneliness, and finds himself listening for the first time in his life for those soft footsteps of Eden. Then his mate nudges his elbow, and asks him if he is feeling all right. He smiles awkwardly, knowing he could never tell them what he has been thinking, nor what he longs for, and goes back to his beer.

For a long time the old man has had a passion for butterflies. Today he is going to one of the best spots he knows. He will pick up a friend on the way. She is

on her own, too. Her husband died two years ago. It
is a warm, sunny day. He picks her up in the car, and
they drive to the coast and park near the end of the
headland. Half an hour later, still following the cliff
path, they start climbing down towards the spot where
a stream flows into the sea, and the flowers grow in
such profusion. It is a good year for butterflies, the
clouded yellows have come in large numbers, and the
flowers will be dancing with them all. The path is
quite steep, and they have to watch their feet. So they
do not notice the mist rolling in from the sea till it is
almost upon them. It falls fast, thick and cold. 'The
butterflies will not fly in this,' they say. Sure enough,
when they reach the stream and the flowers, there are
none at all to be seen. No use waiting. The weather
has turned. What a pity! It will be hours before the
mist lifts.

This time, however, they are wrong. They are nearly
back at the car, when the mist vanishes as quickly as it
came, and the sun shines warm again, and lights up the
grassy bank they are passing. A few orchids are growing
there, and they stop to bend low over one that has just
come into bloom and still has that wonderful fresh,
rich purple of youth. A small butterfly settles two feet
away. It is black, shimmering black, its wings edged
with delicate ivory. For that moment they think they
have never seen anything so exquisite in their whole
lives. The butterfly feeds for a while, then rises high in
the air and is gone. They look at each other. That

night, in their sleep, they hear, as faint as a butterfly's wings in a summer's air, God's feet dancing.

The priest is watching television. It's an old film, black and white. There's a nun in it. A nice nun! A kind, sympathetic, brave nun! The priest thinks it's the first good nun she's ever seen in a film. They're usually the most appalling despots, running schools with rods of iron and doctrines designed to break the wills of the children in their so-called care, or else they are quite impossible and sing daft songs on the tops of mountains. But this nun is both human and good! Like the one she visits every so often in the retreat house the other end of the town. Time she saw her again. She picks up the phone and makes an appointment. A few days later she finds herself sitting in the retreat house garden, talking of how she seems to have lost God in all the palaver of the ritual, of how she feels she is going through the motions, of how she has been preaching about God less and less, and when she does she has this empty feeling in the pit of her soul and a rising sense of hypocrisy in her throat, and how she can tell no-one about it, for they would not understand, or would quickly condemn, except for her, of course, this old friend in the grey habit who always listens, and never sits in high judgement on anyone. The nun smiles ruefully and tells her that unfortunately she finds judging people extremely tempting at times, but then she says it is all very straightforward, and very natural, and that she really has nothing to fear, that God is as close as the air, only closer, as warm as this summer sun on their backs, and that prayer is as simple as conversation, as an enjoyment of each other's company. Never before has the priest entertained the notion that God might enjoy her company. She has not really ever thought of enjoying God's, either. Her God has been too powerful to be *enjoyed*. She touches the nun's hand, gives her a kiss and bids her farewell. As she walks home, she can hear the footsteps of God beside her, and she realizes for the first time how shy God is, and how much love there is between them.

'The young man,' you ask, 'does he have a happy ending, too?' Yes. It takes him a few years, a career in ruins because of drink, and loneliness more terrible than he has ever known. But then he retrains and goes abroad to work with victims of land mines, and there, in that country where every step, it seems, threatens disaster, he finds himself, finds others, and discovers the God he has been listening for for so many years. He hears his slow, halting footsteps every day.

GOD'S PLAY

God looked at all he had made. See! Very good!
(Genesis 1.31)

God looked at the earth. See! Ruined!   (Genesis 6.12)

God went wandering wide over the earth that he had made. The gates of Eden were shut. He did not walk there any more. The Garden was spoiled, and, like Cain, he had become a vagabond and a vagrant upon the face of the earth. What to do, to turn this ruin again to goodness?

One evening he slipped into a wood where badgers lived. The ground was steep, covered with trees, bracken and rhododendron bushes. The air scarcely moved. God waited. For the farmers the day's work was done, and the tractors clanked the carts home along the road at the wood's edge. Pheasants flew into the wood to roost for the night, and started calling loudly. Other birds began singing the borders of their territories before settling down for the night. It was a noisier place than you might have expected, but God did not mind. He waited, quiet as a mouse and quieter still.

The sun disappeared behind the distant hills, and the badgers began to emerge from their sett. Their noses sniffed the air. God looked down on them, smiled, and waited. Still their noses twitched. Suddenly they caught the scent of his glory. They came rushing up the narrow track from the sett towards him. They tumbled about him, yelping with excitement. 'Come and play with us!' they cried, and so he did.

What a night they had! They chased God all over the wood, and he chased them, they played leapfrog over him, and rolled with him down the steep slopes. The other creatures of the wood did not get a wink of sleep. In the end, as the dawn arrived and the sun paled the sky behind the wood, the badgers, tired out, led God towards their sett, and brought him down its tunnels to their chambers in the warm earth. And so God came to live with the badgers, and made his home with them in the warm, red earth, and made it a holy place.

God went wandering wide over the earth that he had made. One morning he went walking upon the surface of the ocean, treading lightly upon the waves, climbing their high ridges and hiding himself in the troughs. He walked on, waiting for the dolphins to find him. Soon they did. They saw him from afar, and came racing towards him. When they reached him, they got up on their tails and danced a hilarious circle-dance around him. God laughed, and splashed the water of the ocean as high as heaven. 'Come and play with us!' the dolphins cried, and so he did.

What a day they had! They went leaping and diving from one side of the ocean to the other. They balanced God on their fins, and flicked him high into the air with their tails. So, as the sun slipped down towards the horizon, and turned the sky to flame, God made his home in the swelling ocean with the dolphins and made it a holy place.

God went wandering wide over the earth that he had made. One afternoon he sat on the edge of a city waiting for the swifts to arrive. They had flown thousands upon thousands upon thousands of miles since last they were in those parts. Never in all those many months had they touched the ground, or found a perch. They had lived all the days and all the nights in the air. They had played in the air, they had fed in the air, they had slept in the air, floating high on its soft bed. Soon they would be back, and they would see God waiting for them, for their eyes were sharp. And so they were, and so they did, and they shot through the air towards him. They split into small parties and went dashing and hurtling around him, screaming their surprise and their delight. 'Come and play with us!' they cried, and so he did.

What a time they had! They flew in such fast, tight circles round the pair of ravens perched on top of the cathedral tower, that they made them dizzy. They flew so low over an old lady hanging out her washing, that she felt the beat of their wings on her face, looked up in surprise and dropped half the clothes on the grass.

And so, when the birds rose high to drift and sleep through the hours of darkness, God made his home in the shining sky with the swifts, and made it a holy place.

God went wandering wide over the earth that he had made. One morning he came to the edge of another town, but this time he walked straight on. The people of the town were hurrying to work, and did not notice him as they passed him by, for their minds were on other things and they were in too much of a rush. God walked on until he came to the gates of a school. He stood outside and waited. The children were still in the playground. Soon it would be time for them to go inside. Then, suddenly, they saw him standing at the gates. They knew about not talking to strangers, but God was no stranger. God was God, and God was welcome! They rushed over to him, grabbed hold of him and pulled him into the playground. 'Come and play with us!' they cried, and so he did.

What a time they had! They taught God all their games, and he taught them the ones he had played with the badgers and the dolphins and the swifts. They chased him through the wood, and hid with him in the warm, red earth. They dived deep in the waters of the sea, and came leaping with him through the curling waves. They flew with him to the top of the sky and back, and went hurtling over the roofs of the school and over the town and fields beyond. You don't believe me? Ask the children. They will tell you!

In the end the children had to stop. They were too tired to go on. 'Come on!' they said to God. 'Playtime's over. Come with us inside our school. We've got a new hall. It's brilliant, really brilliant! Come and see! Come and see!'

And so he did. And that is how God came to make his home in the town, in the children's school, in their bright new hall, and made it a holy place.

GOD'S MUSIC

'Truly I tell you, unless you change and become like
children, you will never enter the kingdom of heaven.'
(Matthew 18.3)

The child was young enough to know that speaking
to God was the most natural thing in all the world, to
know that God laughed and cried, to know that God's
house was not a grand place, but small and intimate,
warm, comfortable and very safe, and that God had
carpet slippers on her feet. She had not yet been
taught to be afraid of God, or that she was not good
enough for her, or that she always had to be on her
best behaviour with her and keep as many secrets
from her as she could. She liked God and liked her
company. It was as simple for her as that.

But the child grew up, and learned she had to be
more sophisticated. Adults told her it was much more
complicated. Adults spoke of guilt, confession and
praise. Adults taught her to be polite with God, to doff
her cap, bend the knee, touch her forelock and watch
her step. Adults filled her silences with words to say
and songs to sing, and those put God on such a high
pedestal that she could not see her any more, let alone
reach to kiss her. In fact, God was no longer for kiss-
ing. Adults taught her that, too. They turned her God
into a 'He' with a large capital 'H', removed His carpet

slippers, and clothed Him with High Dignity.

For a long time the growing child, moving inexorably towards adulthood and then arriving there, believed what she was told. She learned that it was not proper to *like* God. She was to *love* God instead, so long as underneath she was secretly afraid.

Yet the memories of childhood, by the mercy of God, did not leave her entirely. Deep in her mind and soul they still talked softly, producing in her an unease, a holy doubt, a sense of something precious that was lost, and a longing to find it again.

One day she packed her spiritual bags and left. She left behind the people who were content to remain where they were. She left those who were sure they had already arrived, and spoke as if they owned the Promised Land. She abandoned their terrifying certainties, and went out into what they told her was no-man's land, no-woman's land, no-god's land. She tried also, as far as she could, to leave behind those people's fear of God, the fear that lurked beneath their talk of love and praise. A new fear came upon her, the fear of the unknown, the fear of loneliness. She packed that in her bag, along with her unease, her yearning, her holy doubt, and a new sense of adventure and a large exhilaration.

She passed many on the road going in the opposite direction, to the patches of ground she had left behind, to the familiar pieces of territory where all was known and no surprises were to be had.

Yet soon she was not alone. Others came and joined her.

'Don't look so serious!' someone said. 'Can you play anything?'

'A musical instrument, do you mean?'

'Yes.'

'I don't think so.'

'That's a funny answer. Try this.' He put a hand inside his coat and produced a tuba.

'But I can't. I mean I've never . . . How do you blow? I can't read music.'

'Try.'

'But this is ridiculous!'

'Yes, it is. Try.'

She picked up the tuba, cradled it awkwardly in her arms, put it to her lips and blew. She produced a singularly rude noise, and her companions fell about laughing.

'Wonderful!' they cried. 'That'll do. Come on!'

'But I can't do it properly at all!'

'You will. Come on!'

Lugging along the tuba as best she could, she started off again with her companions. They were still laughing. She noticed most of them had musical instruments of one kind or another. One poor man was pushing a piano.

The tuba was very big, and very heavy. 'Some of you aren't carrying anything,' she complained.

'Yes we are,' they replied. 'Our voices.'

'You mean you're the choir?'

'Exactly. You're beginning to understand. We travel light. The adults taught you too well, back there. That's why you're having to drag that great thing along. But we haven't far to go now.'

At the top of the next hill, the ones in the front of the group suddenly stopped.

'Listen to that!' they said.

Beneath them stretched a wide plain, and in the middle of it was the God the woman had set out to find, the God of her childhood. She, her God, out there, in the middle of the plain, was playing a saxophone. Its sound made bright the air, soft, lilting, inviting, sensuous, ethereal, a single instrument weaving together the sounds of heaven and earth and in-between. The woman had never heard anything so wonderful in all her life, nor so beautiful.

She put her lips to the mouthpiece of the tuba. Without hesitation or restraint she began to play a love-song, soft, lilting, inviting, sensuous, ethereal. It filled the plain and wove itself together with the sound of the saxophone.

Her companions took up their own instruments. Slowly they played or sang their way down the long slope onto the plain and out to its centre. By the time they reached God their music had become a romp, enough to wake the angels in their beds. Eventually it subsided again, fell back to a gentle pianissimo, rocked heaven back to sleep, and then, miraculously, became a single thread. All the notes became as one, sound merged with sound and made a single beauty.

In the midst of them God put down her saxophone, listened for a spell, and began to dance.

THE HANDS OF GOD

So the last will be first.   (Matthew 20.16)

The streets of the heavenly city were strangely empty. I hadn't exactly hoped to find God waiting for me at the gates. In fact, I hadn't expected to be there at all, and meeting God was not something I'd been on the edge of my coffin for. I hadn't lived a good life. Been in and out of prison. Never had any time for God, and didn't want to start then. And I'd died too much of a sudden, as well. Hadn't died what you religious people call a good death. Too much pain and too much anger. I'd still been all bitter, and scared stiff, too, when the final breath came – though the stiff bit came later, now I come to think about it.

They hadn't found me for three days.

Nobody had come to my funeral. I'd lost contact with my family years before. None of them knew where I lived, and I didn't know how many of them were alive or dead. Had no friends either. I was never very good at making friends, and worse at keeping them. I'd always made a mess of things. In my last years I'd been all on my own. One of the undertaker people had sat in on the funeral, and someone from the social services had turned up. The vicar had done a good job, considering, but he hadn't seemed too sure of himself when he got onto the subject of my prospects with the Almighty. They'd hoped a neighbour might come, but I'd kept myself too much to myself, hadn't I, and been too much of a nuisance the rest of the time.

I thought it was all because I was abused as a child, but I didn't expect God to agree with that. After all, he knows just how bad we really are, doesn't he. My old Dad taught me that when I was a kid, when he got his strap out, and my Mum said the same when she did those other things with me. I was a bad boy, they said, a bad, bad boy. I believed them, of course. Well, you do, don't you. I never gave up believing them. I died still believing them.

That was why I was more than a bit surprised not to find myself in the other place, down among the teeth-gnashers. After all, I deserved it. But there I was in heaven, in the old heavenly city, inside the gates. Only there weren't any gates, pearly ones or otherwise. That was a surprise as well. No gates. Nowhere to put any gates. No walls, see. Nothing to keep people out.

It was all so quiet, and no-one around! So I thought I'd go for a wander. Felt alright to do that. No notices to say you couldn't, anyway.

It was a sight better than the place where I'd lived, I tell you! It was like coming home, it was; least, like coming to the home I'd always dreamed of as a kid, and not just as a kid either. The sort of home you read about in books, only I'd never read about one like this. And it was *my* home! And God's, of course. *Our* home. Me and him, and lots of others, presumably. Because if I was there, I couldn't think who wasn't.

So where was everyone? It was all very quiet. Until I found it down a side street. God's house.

Now that was a disappointment, at least at first. If you'd asked me what God's house was like, I'd have said it must be enormous and really grand and gold all over, with windows too high up to see into and flights of tall steps and angels guarding the doors, huge doors, banged up shut and too heavy for anyone ordinary to open, so the angels would have to open them for you, only they would only do that if you'd been very good all your life, and I hadn't, so that was that as far as I was concerned, and anyway the place was far too posh, and too frightening an' all, if I was honest, which I rarely was.

But this wasn't like that at all! It was small and ordinary, and the windows were low down, and the door was open and there were angels inside with one of them playing jazz on a piano with the front off and a load of people having the best time of their lives by the sound of it and I didn't know if they would let me in when one of the angels came out and brought me inside and I stood there inside the door feeling a bit of a lemon and my angel had disappeared into the kitchen and I couldn't see God anywhere and I was just going to go back out again when she came out to see me. Just to see *me*! Deliberately! My God was in the middle of making bread, and was up to her elbows in flour, and she came out on purpose, at a tricky stage of the operations, just to see me! I didn't know God wore a pinny! And all of a sudden I remembered my Mum, and I nearly turned and ran. But she came right up to me and gave me a great big hug, like no hug I'd ever had before. I mean it was for me, not just for her. And then she went back to her baking.

And that was my judgement day. I've never been the same since, of course. I'm getting quite good at the jazz, and the baking, with God. And I still have the marks of God's floury hands on my back. Everyone does up here.